GIANT LIZARDS

by Sara Louise

To Delaney,
from one lizard
to another.
fan

Sara Louise Kras
2008

Perfection Learning®

DEDICATION

For my two favorite people—my husband, Joe, and daughter, Julia

ABOUT THE AUTHOR

Sara Louise loves to travel. She has traveled throughout the United States, Canada, Mexico, Africa, Europe, Australia, and Costa Rica. Sara has encountered many beautiful and unusual animals through her travels. Because of this, she has developed a love and fascination for animals.

Sara's goal is to make readers aware of other places, cultures, and creatures. She would like to instill in readers an excitement about the world around them and the adventures that abound.

Cover and book design:
Randy Messer and Deborah Lea Bell

Image Credits: Jeff Foott (www.jfoott.com) pp. 10, 23, 26, 32, 50, 51; Joe Kras pp. 6, 7, 13, 18, 22, 27, 28, 41, 42, 44; Edward Maruska/Cincinatti Zoo pp. 19, 25, 30, 31

Some images copyright www.arttoday.com; Corel pp. 15, 24, 35, 39, 46, 47, 48

Text © 2001 Perfection Learning® Corporation.
All rights reserved. No part of this book may be used or reproduced in any manner whatsoever without written permission from the publisher. Printed in the United States of America. For information, contact Perfection Learning® Corporation, 1000 North Second Avenue, P.O. Box 500, Logan, Iowa 51546-0500.
Tel: 1-800-831-4190 • Fax: 1-712-644-2392

Paperback ISBN 0-7891-5304-1
Cover Craft® ISBN 0-7807-9660-8
4 5 6 7 8 9 PP 10 09 08 07 06 05

CONTENTS

INTRODUCTION

A hot wind blows across the desert. A volcano explodes. It shakes the ground like an earthquake.

A 10-foot **reptile** whips its tongue in and out. It's searching for food.

Where are you? Have you stepped back in time?

You are on Komodo Island. It's south of China in the Indian Ocean. It's near Indonesia.

This is where the largest lizards in the world live. They are the Komodo dragons. The dragons' size is unbelievable. But they share many features with other lizards.

There are nearly 3,750 kinds of lizards in the world. Most are less than 2 feet long. But some grow to be 4 to 7 feet long. Komodo dragons reach a length of 10 feet! These are the giants of the lizard world.

Chapter 1

WHAT IS A LIZARD?

Lizards are reptiles. They are related to snakes, crocodiles, and turtles. Many people think that dinosaurs were lizards' **ancestors**. But that's not the case.

Prehistoric salamanders were their ancestors. But they are not related now.

Salamanders are **amphibians**. That means they live both on land and in water.

Today's lizards are different from salamanders. Lizards have lungs for breathing, dry skin, and eggs with shells.

Lizards have heads, trunks with four legs, and tails. Their legs are at the sides of their bodies. They aren't beneath their bodies like dinosaurs' legs. Most lizards have five clawed toes on each foot.

Lizards usually live in warm climates. They can be found from the driest deserts to **humid** rain forests.

Lizards like warm weather because they are **cold-blooded**. Their body temperatures are controlled by the outside temperature. They usually find warmth from the sun's rays. To keep cool, they look for shade in dark caves or tree trunks. If lizards get too warm or too cold, they won't live.

Temperature is also important to lizards' **digestion**. If lizards eat big meals and their bodies are too hot, the food can't be **digested**. Then the lizards die.

Lizards' blood flow is very poor. This is because their hearts have fewer openings than mammals' hearts. If lizards are too active, they take longer to cool down. They appear lazy because of their slow ways and inactivity. But this is necessary for them to live.

Lizards have ear openings on their heads. Their eardrums are close to the skin. Some lizards hear very well. But they don't hear as well as humans!

Most lizards have eyelids to protect their eyes. Some even have a second set of eyelids. These are **transparent**. They keep wind and sand out of the lizards' eyes.

Some lizards, especially iguanas, have good eyesight. They often use their eyesight to "talk" with one another. Lizards use color to communicate.

During mating, some male lizards' bellies turn electric blue. Or their heads turn bright yellow. This attracts females.

One kind of lizard turns into a rainbow. It has a bright orange head and a violet-blue body. Its tail is orange and black.

After mating, some female lizards keep their eggs in their bodies. This keeps them warm until they hatch. Then the babics are born alive.

Other lizards lay leathery-shelled eggs in nests or holes. There the eggs stay warm until they hatch.

Lizards have tough, scaly skins. The scales are like toenails. Both are made of the same thing. Between these horny scales is soft skin. This lets the lizards bend. Therefore, lizards can walk easily but still be protected. The skin and scales are like suits of armor.

Lizards have glands inside their mouths. These glands sense odors.

Some lizards use their long, flicking tongues to smell. Their tongues carry odors from the air to these glands. Other lizards use their noses to bring air and odors into these glands.

Most lizards have tails longer than their bodies. Many tails have several breaking points.

Sometimes **predators** grab lizards by their tails. The tails snap off. But they still wiggle as though attached. This **distracts** the predators long enough for the lizards to escape. Then the lizards grow new tails!

Often lizards stand on their two back feet. Then they use their tails for balance.

Large lizards also use their tails like clubs. They are used for protection. Or the lizards might use them when fighting other lizards. Hits from swinging tails leave deep cuts.

Lizards' diets vary. They eat anything from fruits and leaves to insects and fish.

The Komodo dragons are the largest lizards. They have even been known to kill and eat water buffalo as big as cows!

Chapter 2

MONITOR LIZARDS

The young 6-foot monitor neared the older 7-foot monitor. The young lizard was aware that it had entered the older one's territory.

The older monitor hissed a warning. It raised up on its back feet. The younger monitor stood up too. It grabbed the older lizard by the neck.

Hugging each other, they swayed back and forth. Finally, the older monitor tripped the other lizard. It fell backward. Then it hissed a defeat. It ran out of the territory.

Monitor lizards are relatives of sea reptiles of long ago. They were called *mosasaurs.*

Mosasaurs had crocodilelike bodies and flippers instead of legs. Their bodies reached lengths of 30 feet.

Their jaws were long. They had sharp, pointed teeth. Mosasaurs had disconnecting jaws. The jaws could come apart where they were joined. Then the lizards could open their mouths very wide to swallow fish whole. Monitor lizards today have this type of jaw.

There are 30 kinds of monitor lizards. They are **tropical** reptiles. Monitors are found in India, Africa, and in some parts of Asia. All of them are fierce meat-eaters.

The Komodo dragon is the largest. Three other large monitors are the water, the Nile, and the white-throated monitors. They reach from 5 to 8 feet in length.

Monitors eat many things. Young monitors eat insects, worms, and eggs. As the lizards grow, they attack snakes, birds, small monkeys, and water rats.

They grab the prey with their teeth. These teeth are sharp and bent slightly backward. The jaws of monitor lizards are very powerful.

Their legs have strong muscles with sharp claws. They use their legs and claws for climbing trees, digging the ground, defending themselves, and tearing at their prey.

Females lay their eggs below the ground. And sometimes they use the hollows of trees.

WHITE-THROATED MONITOR

White-throated monitors grow up to 5½ feet long. That's almost the size of an adult human.

These lizards live in the dry desert areas of Africa. Food is scarce. Females have been known to roam 4 miles in search of food. Males will walk up to 10 miles a day just to find food!

The rainy season is November through March. During this time, these lizards **gorge** themselves. It's common for one monitor to eat 100 snails or 200 grasshoppers in a day.

By May, rain and food become memories. Now the lizards slow down to save energy.

Once, a male lizard was seen in the same tree for two months. It seemed to move from branch to branch. But it never left the tree. It was saving its energy!

WATER MONITOR

Sailors have spotted water monitors off the coast of India. The lizards were many miles out to sea.

These 7- to 8-foot monitors swim through ocean waters with ease. They tuck their legs close to their bodies. Then they use their long tails to steer and move them.

Water monitors catch fish underwater. They stay underwater up to an hour. Then they come to the surface. They use nostrils, set high on their snouts, to breathe.

These monitors are as much at home on land as they are in the water. They are found on coasts and in waters from India to the islands of the Pacific.

NILE MONITOR

Nile monitors live near lakes and rivers in Africa. They dig burrows into the banks. The burrows have many underwater entrances.

Nile monitors often raid crocodiles' nests. They are looking for eggs. But they

must be careful. If female crocodiles find monitors robbing their nests, they will turn the monitors into quick meals!

After mating, females tear holes in termite mounds. Then they lay their eggs. The termites soon patch the holes, leaving the eggs inside.

The nests are the perfect temperature and humidity. When the eggs hatch, baby Nile monitors dig their way out.

Chapter 3

KOMODO DRAGONS

It was 1910. The Dutch pilot's plane crashed into Indonesian waters. He swam to the shore of Komodo Island.

A short time later, he found that giant monsters lived on the island. Luckily, he was able to radio for help. And he was rescued.

Back home, the pilot told stories of the "giant reptiles." But no one believed him.

Everyone knew that dragons didn't exist. But the pilot insisted.

Later, an army officer went to the island. He found that the stories were true.

Many years ago, the nearby Indonesians sent their **outcasts** to the island. They knew the man-eating lizards had powerful jaws. So, soon the outcasts would be dinner!

This no longer happens. Today, a small settlement stands on the island. It's called Komodo Village. The villagers make their living from tourists and fishing.

Today, thousands of visitors tour the island and other nearby islands. They want to see these huge monitor lizards.

Komodo dragons do not usually eat people. But sometimes they are hungry. And prey is hard to find. Then the dragons will attack and eat humans—adults or children.

The villagers are quite aware of the danger. So they stay back if a dragon walks through the village.

Komodo dragons are the largest lizards in the world. Their gray, spotted bodies grow up to 10 feet long. Some weigh up to 365 pounds.

Komodos can run up to 15 miles per hour. That is about the speed of someone riding a bike.

Komodos have an amazing sense of smell. They smell with their forked tongues.

Dragons use their tongues to smell prey. They turn their heads left and right as they walk. They constantly flick their tongues to sense the prey.

They are able to smell things very far away. Then they run to reach the prey quickly.

An adult Komodo usually eats pigs, goats, deer, young buffalo, and horses. Komodos even eat other dragons or their eggs.

When hunting, Komodos lie flat in bushes and wait near trails. They watch for pigs or deer. As the prey passes, Komodos rush out. They bring their prey to the ground with their strong bodies.

The dragons can almost swallow their prey whole.

Komodo dragons' jaws are unusual. They are similar to snakes' jaws. Their jaws sometimes become unhooked when the dragons are eating. This makes it easy to eat large prey. Even larger than themselves!

Komodos can sense if another animal is hurt. A hurt animal is an easy meal.

This is one reason Komodo dragons avoid one another. Fights between dragons could leave one badly hurt. Then it's a quick dinner for the winner.

Komodos are also known to be **scavengers**. They have been seen walking slowly along the beaches. They are looking for dead fish or animals.

Even though Komodos avoid one another, they often share a meal. And they have done so peacefully.

Dragons eat very quickly. They have sharp, curved teeth. These are perfect for grabbing and cutting meat.

Dragons also **salivate** a lot while eating. This helps them digest large chunks of meat.

Sometimes the **saliva** turns bloody. The blood comes from the spongy skin of their gums. Their gums are often cut by their razor-sharp teeth.

Komodo dragons' bites are deadly. The saliva contains **bacteria**. Bitten animals sometimes escape the dragons. But they soon become ill and die.

Komodos are at home on land and in the water. They are sometimes referred to as "land crocodiles."

These lizards are good swimmers. They use their tails to steer themselves. If a bad storm hits their island, they swim to other islands for safety.

Komodos often dive too. They go as deep as 6 feet looking for dead animals.

Komodos live in caves dug by other animals or themselves. They dig with their front feet.

After mating, female Komodos dig U-shaped burrows. They lay their eggs at the ends. This provides protection for the eggs and the newborn Komodos. They are out of reach to passing hungry Komodo dragons.

The females lay between 20 and 40 eggs. This happens over a period of several weeks.

The eggs develop for eight months. During this time, they are in constant danger of being eaten by other dragons.

Once hatched, the baby Komodos range in size from 8 to 19 inches long. Young lizards feed on insects and smaller lizards.

Many young Komodos live in trees to escape the larger adult Komodos. Adult bodies are too big and bulky to climb trees.

The little lizards are orange and yellow with black and white markings. This makes them very hard to see in the trees.

Chapter 4

TEIID LIZARDS

A hungry 4-foot tegu lizard neared the farm with caution. It smelled the chickens and their eggs. This gave the lizard the courage to approach the shack.

The chickens squawked noisily. They flew, dodging the large lizard. The lizard grabbed a chicken by the head, crushing its skull.

Hearing human voices, the tegu turned and ran. It dragged the dead chicken in its powerful jaws.

Bullets hit the ground near the tegu's body. But it continued to run. It zigzagged along the ground, dodging the flying bullets.

Tegus are members of the teiid lizard family. These lizards are known for their speed. They have long bodies with muscular legs and long round tails. Their smooth-looking scales are small and circular.

Teiids also have long forked tongues. Like monitor lizards, they use their tongues to smell prey. Most teiids live in South America.

TEGU

Tegus are big lizards. They live in the subtropical regions of South America. They always live near lakes or rivers.

Tegus are excellent swimmers. The word *tegu* means "lizard" in a language that began along the Amazon River.

Tegus grow up to 6 feet in length. They are dark brown or black. Small white or yellowish groups of spots appear in bands on their bodies. Their bellies are a cream color.

Tegus are known for their strength and quickness. These lizards are very aggressive.

Tegus like to eat many things. Young tegus eat a variety of spiders, snails, and earthworms.

Older tegus have bigger teeth. And their jaw muscles are more developed. This makes it possible for them to eat fruit, frogs, snakes, chickens, and eggs.

Tegus are aggressive hunters. They trap their prey in their mouths. Then they hit their prey several times on the ground.

This tears the prey and makes it easier to swallow.

Mating season begins at the end of November. After mating, the females build caves in high places. Then they lay white oval eggs. Or sometimes females lay their eggs in termite mounds.

When the tegus are born, they are about 3 inches long. They are bright green with black spots. They feed on insects seconds after being born.

CAIMAN LIZARD

Caiman lizards are part of the teiid family in South America. They live near the Amazon River. There the land is soft and marshy.

Caiman lizards grow up to 4 feet long. They were named for the scales on their backs. These scales look like scales from *caimans*, or alligators.

During the spring, the Amazon River floods the rain forest. Therefore, caiman lizards spend much of their time underwater. They dive deep into the water to find and gather snails and mussels in their mouths.

Over time, these lizards have developed large, rounded teeth to crush the shells. When the lizards surface, they tip back their heads. The snails in their mouths roll back to the crushing teeth.

The teeth break the shells. The lizards eat the insides. Then they spit out the hard shells.

Chapter 5

COMMON IGUANAS

On a sandy beach in Costa Rica in Central America, the iguana smelled meat. The lizard crept quietly up to the girl. She was asleep on the beach.

A beach bag lay next to the girl. The iguana poked its head into it. It grabbed the sandwich with its sharp teeth.

The girl sat straight up and screamed. The iguana ran for the trees. Up it climbed like a squirrel. The sandwich meat hung from its mouth.

Iguanas live in South and Central America, Mexico, and Texas. There are about 400 different types of iguanas. Iguanas vary in size. Common iguanas are the largest.

Common iguanas are about 6 feet long. They love to bask in the sun.

A large scaly fringe runs from the tops of their heads to the ends of their tails. The fringe gets smaller the closer it gets to the tail. These lizards look like mythical dragons of long ago.

Under their chins, common iguanas have loose flaps of skin called *dewlaps.* These flaps are used to signal other iguanas. Dewlaps inflate when iguanas challenge other males or try to attract mates.

Common iguanas usually stay high in the trees of tropical jungles. These lizards often live in holes in the trees.

Common iguanas mainly eat the trees' fruit, leaves, or flowers. Hibiscus flowers are a favorite food.

Iguanas' small, sharp teeth help them to tear apart large leaves. This makes the leaves easier to swallow. Iguanas also eat many types of insects for protein.

Despite their size, iguanas are fast runners. On the ground they are faster than dogs. They also can climb trees as quickly as squirrels. And they can jump from high places without being hurt.

Iguanas' nails are long and sharp. They use these nails to defend themselves from their enemies. They also use their tails as weapons. Their tails give quite a blow!

These lizards are excellent swimmers.

Iguanas' tails are used to steer the lizards underwater. When they swim, their front and back legs are pressed against their bodies. This makes them **streamlined**.

During courtships or fights, iguanas push up on their front legs and bob up and down. They look as though they're doing push-ups.

Also during courtships, many males are more colorful than the females. They use their colors to impress and attract possible mates.

Usually the females lay their eggs in holes in the ground or under logs. Then the females leave. When the babies hatch, they take care of themselves!

Common iguanas are sometimes referred to as "tree chickens." It's not uncommon to find their tender white meat on dinner tables. In some places, common iguanas are raised for food.

Chapter 6

DRAGONS OF THE GALAPAGOS ISLANDS

A volcano exploded. Rivers of molten lava flowed down its side. The lava sizzled as it hit the seawater.

The marine iguana steered clear of the boiling water around the lava flow. It nimbly ate seaweed from the rocks on the ocean floor.

Waves crashed over its green-gray body. It swayed with the tide. It used its thick claws to keep it from floating away.

The lizard had been in the water for more than an hour. Its body temperature was dangerously low.

The iguana climbed the slimy cliff to join the rest of its herd. Climbing over several other iguanas, it found a resting spot to sunbathe. The iguana cleared its nose of any saltwater or seaweed by spitting a salty vapor from its nostrils.

The Galapagos Islands are off the west coast of South America. They are home to marine iguanas and land iguanas. Both are about 4 feet in length.

MARINE IGUANA

Marine iguanas live in large colonies. They are found along the shores of the Galapagos Islands.

Their entire diet consists of algae and seaweed found on the ocean floor. Small fish hover around while the iguanas are eating. The fish are looking for tiny sea life that is stirred up by the iguanas.

Marine iguanas sometimes dive as deep as 50 feet to have a meal. But they can only stay underwater for 10 minutes. Then they must come back up for air.

LAND IGUANA

Female land iguanas climb 4,000-foot volcanic mountains to lay their eggs. This hike takes them 10 days to accomplish.

Steam from the volcano vents keeps the ash below the ground at about 90°F. This is perfect for keeping iguana eggs warm.

Rocks often fall around the females as they climb down into the volcano. Many female iguanas are killed.

They dodge falling rocks and slide down into the large crater. Once at the bottom, they fight one another for places to lay their eggs.

After 100 days, the gray-white, tiger-striped hatchlings come out from the ground. Hawks and snakes wait hungrily to snatch them.

The hatchlings sense danger. They run in groups. Some become food. But some escape. They climb the crater wall. Then they walk 10 miles to where the land iguanas live.

The land on the Galapagos Islands is very dry and harsh. These lizards have very little plant life for food. They have **adapted** by eating cacti—spines and all!

Chapter 7

GIANTS IN THE LIZARD WORLD

Iguanas, Komodo dragons, monitor lizards, and teiid lizards are the giants. They have adopted unusual ways of living.

Their thick suits of armor, muscular bodies, whiplike tails, and sharp, pointed teeth make them look like roaming lost dinosaurs. These giants of the lizard world seem lost in time. But they have found a place in the modern world.

GLOSSARY

adapt   to change in order to live under specific conditions

amphibian   cold-blooded animal that has gills and lives in water when young and is air-breathing as an adult

ancestor   very old relative

bacteria   very tiny organisms that sometimes cause illness and death

cold-blooded   having a body temperature that depends on the air temperature of surroundings

digest   to break down food to be used by the body

digestion   body's way of breaking down food to be used by the body

distract   to direct attention to something else

gorge   to eat greedily; to stuff with food

humid	containing heavy amounts of moisture
outcast	one who is sent away by society for being unacceptable
predator	animal that hunts other animals for food
prehistoric	relating to times before written history
reptile	cold-blooded, air-breathing animal that crawls on its belly or on short legs
saliva	watery substance in the mouth that aids in digestion
salivate	to have saliva flowing in the mouth
scavenger	animal that eats other animals that are already dead
streamline	make easy for moving
transparent	thin enough to see through
tropical	living in a hot, rainy area